If My Depression Had a Name

An Illustrated Poem

Written By: Jennifer C. Williams

Illustrated By: Phillip "Maikeru" Ross

If My Depression Had a Name: An Illustrated Poem

Illustrations by Phillip "Maikeru" Ross

Published by Playtime Kids An imprint of SONshines and Playtime LLC Upper Marlboro, Maryland

Library of Congress Control Number: 2026944930

ISBN 979-8-9956119-0-5 (Paperback)
ISBN 979-8-9956119-1-2 (Hardcover)
ISBN 979-8-9956119-2-9 (Ebook)
First Edition, 2026
Printed in the United States of America
sonshinesandplaytime.com

DEDICATION

**To my husband Stephen, and my boys, Nico and Gabriel,
for always making me feel seen
and for making every day a great day to have a great day!**

HI, BOB.

If my depression had a name,
it would be BOB.

HI, BOB.

If my depression

had a sound,

it would be **BOOM.**

It would be quiet,

then suddenly LOUD,

then quiet again.

If my depression had a voice, it would be SMALL and MOUSE-LIKE, so small no one else would hear it.

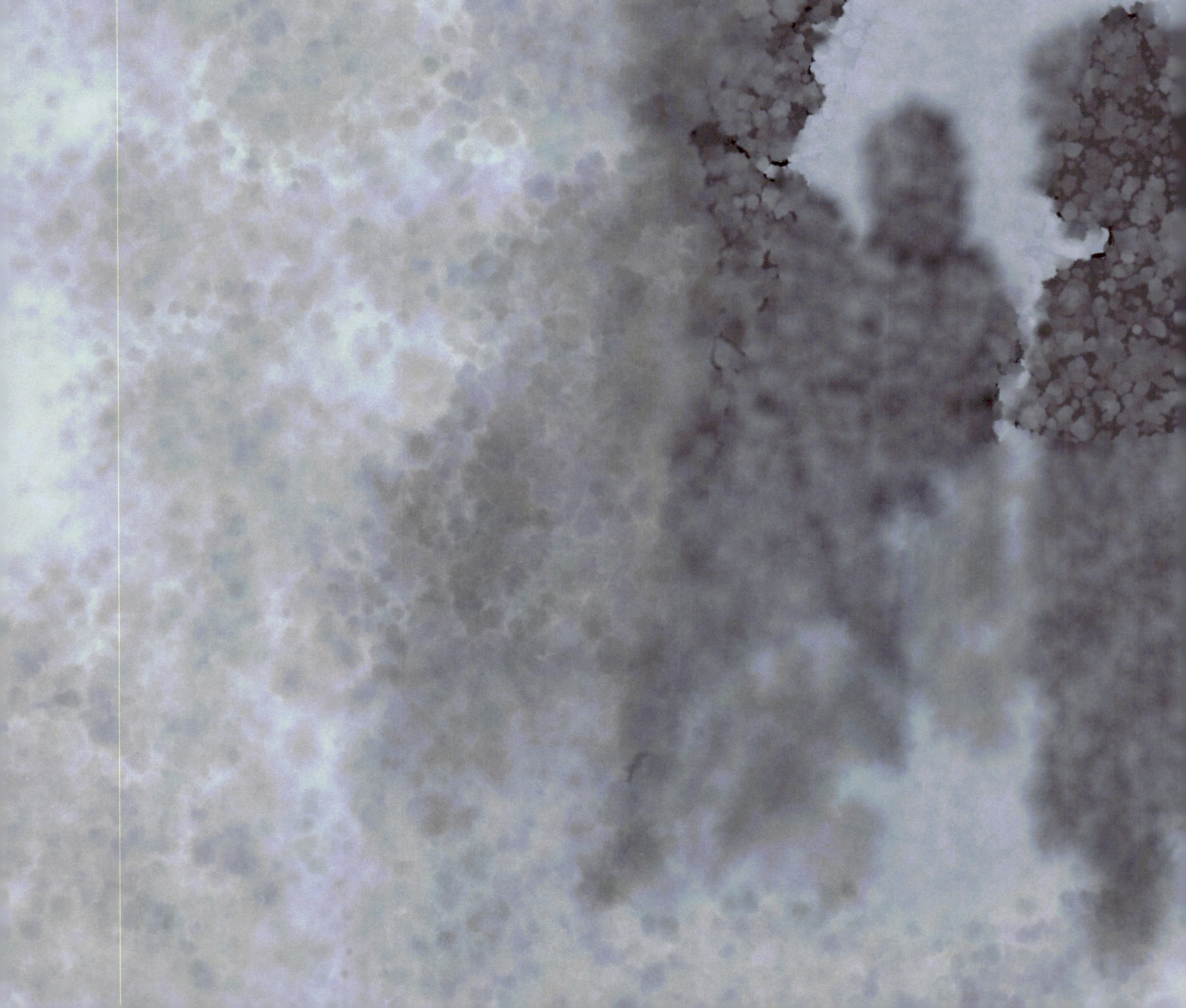

If my depression had a face,
it would be invisible to others,
but I would know it was **BLUE**.

If my depression had a feeling,
it would be SADNESS,
cosplaying as HAPPY.

If my depression had a stomach,
it would HURT.

It would really, really HURT.

If my depression had eyes,
they would stay closed,
and all you would see would be TEARS.

If my depression could move, it would STAY STILL.

But if my depression could talk,
I would finally speak,
and I would feel relief
in telling someone I trusted
how **HEAVY** it feels for me.

If my depression had a hand,
I would slowly let it go.

I WOULD TAKE A SLOW DEEP BREATH
AND WATCH IT WALK AWAY FROM ME.

If my depression left, I would feel FREE, because I would no longer confuse Bob for me.

I could finally just be **ME**.

A NOTE FROM JENNIFER

Hey reader,

Before you close this book, I want to tell you something I tell the kids who come into my therapy office. Every story you love is a hero's journey. Spider-Man. Moana. Black Panther. They all start somewhere ordinary, get pulled into something hard, and come out the other side more themselves than they were before.

You just read about a boy who did something brave. He did not save the world. He did something quieter and, in a lot of ways, harder. He noticed Bob. He gave him a name. He stopped pretending he was fine. He told someone. He chose himself. Just because his journey happens inside his body and his mind does not make it smaller. It makes it brave.

I am a therapist. I have sat with a lot of kids who felt exactly like the boy in this book.

Here is what I know about depression:

Depression lies. It tells you that you are alone. You are not.

Depression is scary. It can show up out of nowhere and make everything feel harder than it should be.

Depression feels fuzzy. Like there is a fog between you and the rest of your life.

And sometimes it feels like no one else will understand. Someone will. There is always someone.

Depression is something you are carrying. It is not who you are. You are still you underneath it. The weight of depression feels heavy, but I know you can put it down. It might take time. It might take a trusted adult, a friend, a school counselor, or 988, where someone is waiting to talk or text with you any time, day or night. Trust that you can put it down. And when you do, the person standing there is you. The real you. The you that you know. The you that was always there. The hardest part of any hero's journey is the part where you decide to begin. You just did.

I am proud of you.

You are special.

With care,

Jennifer

Jennifer C. Williams, LCPC, PMH-C

About The Author

Jennifer C. Williams, LCPC, PMH-C, is a licensed clinical professional counselor and certified perinatal mental health specialist with two decades of clinical practice. She holds active clinical licensure in Maryland, Washington DC, Virginia, and Florida.

Jennifer is the founder of Pass Go! Therapy and Coaching, a virtual mental health practice focusing on individuals, couples, perinatal mental health, family relationships, and corporate wellness programs. She is also the founder of SONshines and Playtime, a family lifestyle brand built to help parents raise kids who are Curious, Adventurous, Resilient, and Emotionally Intelligent. The capital SON in the brand name is a tribute to her two sons who remind her that everyday is an adventure. Jennifer believes that children deserve to have fun, be playful, curious, joyful, and fully themselves.

She wrote this book because she has spent years watching kids carry feelings they cannot name. She believes giving children the words for hard emotions is one of the most powerful things adults can do.
Jennifer lives in Maryland with her family. Her motto, in her practice and at home, is the same.

"Every day is a great day to have a great day."

ABOUT THE ILLUSTRATOR

Phillip Michael Ross, also known creatively as Maikeru, is a Richmond, Virginia-based multidisciplinary illustrator, designer, and art director with over a decade of experience in visual storytelling. His work blends emotion, atmosphere, culture, and character-driven imagery across editorial design, illustration, branding, and publishing. As an artist, Maikeru focuses on creating visuals that feel human, expressive, and intentional—using color, composition, and body language to tell stories that connect with real people.

Being the illustrator of ***If My Depression Had a Name***, Maikeru brings care, cultural sensitivity, and emotional honesty to a story created to help young readers feel seen, understood, and less alone. As a father, Maikeru approaches stories for children with a deeper sense of responsibility, empathy, and care. His creative work often centers on identity, emotion, and the quiet moments people do not always know how to explain out loud. Whether he is designing a visual system, illustrating a character, or building a full narrative world, his goal is to create work that feels honest, grounded, and meaningful—especially for young readers who deserve to recognize themselves in the stories they hold.

A Note to Caregivers

For the parents, grandparents, and adults reading alongside their child:

Hey Caregiver,

The fact that you picked up this book already tells me something about you. You are paying attention. You are trying. That matters more than you know. You are not failing because your child is struggling. You are loving them well by being right here, right now.

How to Read It Together

Read it yourself first. That way, you have already met Bob before your child does. Then read it together, out loud. Go slowly. Let pauses sit. Silence after a hard line is okay. That silence is the book doing its job.

Do not problem-solve right away. Let the last page rest. Leave the book somewhere your child can return to it on their own if he/she chooses to. Some kids talk right away. Some kids need three days. Both are normal.

Conversation Starters

Right after reading:

- Which line felt most true to you?
- If you had to give your hardest feeling a name, what would you call it?

Is there a feeling you carry that other people cannot see?

A day or two later:

- I have been thinking about that book we read. Did you have any more thoughts about it? How are you doing?
- If your feelings ever get too heavy to carry alone, I am always available as the first person to call.

If Your Child Shares Something Hard

Breathe. You do not need all the answers right away.

Say: Thank you for telling me. I hear you. Tell me more. Your feelings make sense. We will figure this out together.

Skip: Why didn't you tell me sooner. You have nothing to be sad about. Just cheer up. Other kids have it worse.

If your child mentions wanting to hurt themselves, reach out to a licensed mental health provider, your pediatrician, or **call or text 988**. Trust your gut. You know your child.

You are the safe place. This book is just a tool.

Jennifer C. Williams, LCPC, PMH-C | passgolife.com | sonshinesandplaytime.com

Parent Resource

Scan Here

A Note for Counselors and Educators

For the school counselors, therapists, teachers, and SEL professionals using this book
Thank you for the work you do. You sit with children in the hardest moments of their day, and you do it with limited time, limited resources, and limited backup. This book was written to be a tool you can actually use.

What This Book Does Clinically

If My Depression Had a Name is a developmentally appropriate externalization story for children ages 9 to 14. Naming Bob is the therapeutic mechanism. When a child gives a feeling a name, they create the distance needed to talk about it without being consumed by it. The story models help-seeking behavior, and parts work, without prescribing it, which respects the child's agency while opening the door.

This is not a diagnostic tool. It is a conversation tool.

How to Use It in Your Setting

In a counseling office:
- Read it together during a session and pause after Bob is named. Ask the child what they would name their hardest feeling.
- Use it as a warm-up for children who are not yet ready to talk directly about their internal experience.
- Reference Bob in later sessions as shared language. "Has Bob been around this week?" lands easier than "Are you depressed?"

In a classroom or SEL block:
- Read it aloud as part of a social-emotional learning unit on identifying and naming emotions.
- Pair it with a feelings-naming activity. Invite students to write or draw what they would call their hardest feeling.
- Use it during Mental Health Awareness Month or any unit on emotional literacy.

In a school counseling office:
- Keep a copy in your waiting area. Some children will pick it up before they say a word.
- Send a copy home with families who need a gentle entry point into a conversation they do not know how to start.
- Use it during parent meetings to model the language you want families to bring into the home.

A Note on Disclosure

If a child discloses suicidal ideation, self-harm, or abuse while you are reading this book together, follow your professional protocol and mandated reporting requirements. Document what was said in the child's own words. Connect with caregivers per your district or agency policy. The book is not a substitute for crisis assessment, safety planning, or your clinical judgment.

Bulk Orders and Institutional Pricing

This book is available in softcover and hardcover through Amazon, IngramSpark, Barnes and Noble, and sonshinesandplaytime.com. Bulk pricing is available for schools, counseling offices, libraries, and SEL programs. For institutional orders, professional development collaborations, or speaking inquiries, please reach out directly.

Thank you for choosing this book for the children you serve. They are lucky to have you in the room.

Clinical Resource

Scan Here

Jennifer C. Williams, LCPC, PMH-C

sonshinesandplaytime.com | passgolife.com

NOW IT'S YOUR TURN!

DRAW AND NAME A FEELING THAT YOU HAVE.

www.ingramcontent.com/pod-product-compliance
Lightning Source LLC
LaVergne TN
LVHW070937210926
848482LV00003B/261
9798995611905